lullabies FOR THE *insomniacs*

lullabies for the insomniacs

A MEMOIR IN VERSE

ELLA GRACE FOUTZ

Zest Books™
An imprint of Lerner Publishing Group, Inc.
241 First Avenue North
Minneapolis, MN 55401 USA

For reading levels and more information, look up this title at www.lernerbooks.com.
Visit us at zestbooks.net.

Cover and interior illustrations by Bárbara Tamilin

Designed by Athena Currier
Main body text set in Janson Text LT Std
Typeface provided by Adobe Systems

Library of Congress Cataloging-in-Publication Data

Names: Foutz, Ella Grace, author.
Title: Lullabies for the insomniacs : a memoir / Ella Grace Foutz.
Description: Minneapolis : Zest Books, 2025. | Audience term: juvenile | Audience: Ages 13–18 Zest Books | Audience: Grades 10–12 Zest Books | Summary: "A teen with bipolar disorder fights for survival and self-understanding in Ella Grace Foutz's memoir in verse, balancing poignancy with moments of levity as Foutz navigates the complex terrain of mental illness and mental health"— Provided by publisher.
Identifiers: LCCN 2024052576 (print) | LCCN 2024052577 (ebook) | ISBN 9798765671290 (library binding) | ISBN 9798765671306 (paperback) | ISBN 9798765683156 (epub)
Subjects: LCSH: Foutz, Ella Grace—Juvenile literature. | Bipolar disorder—Juvenile literature. | Bipolar disorder—Patients—Biography—Juvenile literature. | LCGFT: Autobiographies
Classification: LCC RJ506.D4 F68 2025 (print) | LCC RJ506.D4 (ebook) | DDC 616.8950092 [B]—dc23/eng20250505

LC record available at https://lccn.loc.gov/2024052576
LC ebook record available at https://lccn.loc.gov/2024052577

Manufactured in the United States of America
1-1012040-54156-4/2/2025

A Note to Readers

This book involves discussions of suicidal ideation and references to suicide and disordered eating. If you are experiencing thoughts of suicide, have any questions about suicide, are worried about a loved one and seeking guidance, or simply need a listening ear, you can call or text 988 for confidential, anonymous support.

For Ben.

For Papa.

And to my sixteen-year-old self,
who I wasn't there for,
for whom I should have been,
who I know is still out there,
and whom I am trying to be there for
Now.

Table of Contents

I.

time zones

Bipolar.

What is that supposed to mean?

Literally:
Two poles.

Two poles of what?

The Earth?
North and South?
magnetic fields
holding a planet together
The edge of the light paved between them
and the shadow behind
the sweep of the sun spilling
across the surface
Time zones
a circular spectrum of light to dark

That's what group therapy is like.
A spectrum of light to dark.
The phases of day to night
strung in a circle of chairs.
There's me,
who you wouldn't know
if you didn't know.
And then there's Nora,
who says some starkly shaded things
but with a smile
with inflection

with an arm full of rubber bracelets
and then there's Adam—
who does not say dark things
but the words he does say
are never colored-in.
It's like they were outlined
but he gave up on each drawing
before he got to the crayons

and then there's Cassandra.
And just nothing.
Silence.
She's folded up inside
her chair
grimacing at the carpet
like the fluorescent lights
hurt her eyes.
They ask her questions.
She shakes her head at each one.

She's mad they forced her to stay alive.

And some part of me can't help but think
How to defy time
before the next phase of light
or lack thereof
reaches my time zone,
How to keep the light inside
when the next hour reaches me
How to hold the sun in my hands
How to keep the light from slipping
How to defy time—

Oh how our eyes adjust to the light,
the lack.
My twilight would be their daybreak.

A year later,
my psychiatrist would tell me that depression
is just a spectrum of genes.
She made a line in the air with her hands.
Everyone is on the spectrum somewhere.
Everyone has some genes for the dark.
Some have lighter genes than others. Or basically,
Time is relative.

Bipolar disorder is not "mood swings."
It's okay.
That's what I thought too.
That's why I took years to realize I had it.
Bipolar is just time zones.
It's just nighttime.

Regularly.

Mania

is an astral plane
that you can visit by untying your spirit
from your body
and you can go and touch the constellations
and watch the cosmos crash like tides
from a seat
In the sky
harvest wishes from the stars
make friends
with ghosts and supernovas

Just Don't Get Lost.
Don't forget
where you left yourself behind
in reality, in that other sphere
because There Are Demons
in that astral plane
who pick up warm skins
like hermit crabs trading shells
and they will steal your body from you
and It Is Not Fun
being trapped inside yourself beside one.

Depression

is sharing breaths
with something
you are not.

Recurring

When I was little I had this recurring nightmare
where I am locked in a car that starts speeding off
of its own accord.
I watch the speedometer climb.
I watch a world that is perfectly still
flash by like it's running away
and nothing is going to stop me
I don't know how to drive a car
I am only three or four
steering broken
brakes broken
locks buried
just momentum
just physics
just the laws of the universe
just the vacuum
there are stop signs
there are signs telling me there are stop signs
I rip past them—

It's not crashing that scares me.

To crash is mercy.
After each episode,
while I soak in the darkness
that follows every dream
I am terrified knowing
that in the dream that extends beyond my waking
the car never stops,
and I am carried far, far away
to where I will never find my way back home.

"I Couldn't Sleep Last Night."

You're crazy, you stayed up all night?
(Yes, I know I'm crazy, thank you)
You skipped classes and didn't get a nap?

Maybe you don't understand what Couldn't is?

Here. I'll explain.

It's the difference between holding your breath
and being suffocated.
It's the difference between skipping breakfast
and famine. A camp survivor
said that you don't know what hunger is until you would
Sell Your Soul
for a potato,
And you don't know what tired is until I don't know
what I wouldn't sell to
Sleep,
Oh my goodness please if I could just *sleep*
Oh my goodness please please please
because it's not just last night, it has been
Three,
it is going on
Four,
I am terrified it will be more
Have you ever gone a month without food because you can go three and still live but legends pray tell you can't go two weeks without Sleep I know because I looked it up it terrifies me it's irrational but it's not and like all Needs you take it for granted until you can't have it and you do take it for granted, there are

Four things you need to just Survive, Food and Water and Air and not even to Be Human, just to Be Alive, just to survive often left off the list is the one that you take for granted because unlike Food and Water and the blessed Air you don't need anything on the outside of yourself to

Sleep.
You just need yourself.
But I don't know where myself has gone.

Myself.

Myselfmyselfmyselfmyselfmyselfmyselfmyselfmyselfmysel
fmyselfmyselfmyselfmyselfmyselfmyselfmyselfmyselfmyse
lfmyselfmyselfmyselfmyselfmyselfmyselfmyselfmyselfmy
selfmyselfmyselfmyselfmyselfmyselfmyselfmyselfmyselfm
yselfmyselfmyselfmyselfmyselfmyselfmyselfmyselfmysel
fmyselfmyselfmyselfmyselfmyselfmyselfmyselfmyselfm
yselfmyselfmyselfmyselfmyselfmyselfmyselfmyselfmyse
lfmyselfmyselfmyselfmyselfmyselfmyselfmyselfmyselfmy
selfmyselfmyselfmyselfmyselfmyselfmyselfmyselfmyselfmym
yselfmyselfmyselfmyselfmyselfmyselfmyselfmyselfmysel
fmyselfmyselfmyselfmyselfmyselfmyselfmyselfmyselfmysel
fmyselfmyselfmyselfmyselfmyselfmyselfmyselfmyselfmyself
myselfmyselfmyselfmyselfmyselfmyselfmyselfmyselfmys
elfmyselfmyselfmyselfmyselfmyselfmyselfmyselfmyselfmy
selfmyselfmyselfmyselfmyselfmyselfmyselfmyselfmyself
myselfmyselfmyselfmyselfmyselfmyselfmyselfmyselfmy
selfmyselfmyselfmyselfmyselfmyselfmyselfmyselfmysel
fmyselfmyselfmyselfmyselfmyelfmyselfmyselfmyselfmyself
myselfmyselfmyselfmyselfmyselfmyselfmyselfmyselfmysel
fmyselfmyselfmyselfmyselfmyselfmyselfmyself myself my self

my self my self myself my self my self my self my self my
my self my self my self my self my self my self my self
my self my self my self my self my self my self my
self my self my self my self my self my self
my self my selfmy self my self my self
my self my self myself my self my self my
self my self my self m y s e l f my self
my self my self my self my self
my self my self my self my
selfmy self my self my

my self my self my self

my self my selfmy
self my
self
my

self

my

self

my

self.

My Self
Feels far away.
My skull
Feels fragile
At 4 a.m.
When I grip it
With both hands
And bite a scream
In the dark

And years later
I still think about that.
I think about the night before the morning
We went
I think about my fingertips
Clenching my scalp as hard as they could
And Mom telling me to stay calm
And I wonder whether the grip
Of my hands
Was to harm
Or to protect

From what might

What's funny

Is that looking back,
That special kind of insanity
Is both so gargantuan against the insanity I have now
The insanity I have now is so so miniature

And yet, I remember thinking clearly
As I made the decision to go
How mundane it all was
And was I being melodramatic
Because this
This here by far
Was not the worst of it.

The Morning We Went to the Psych Ward

In real time, I know that
that drive
was one full
of us both being starving
and both neglecting the protein shake in the cup holder
and Mom watching the road
and trying not to let me see
how every night I haven't slept she hasn't either
how bone-deep nervous she was too
and my body scraping for homeostasis
as I lay back in the seat
still not sleeping,
and everything was an unholy sort of unknown

But in the memory that plays in my head,
mostly what I remember is

The blue morning sky.
That I watched grow from its infancy.
Stretching across a highway
empty of a world still waking
and virgin daylight,
swelling through the car window
like cello strings in the hero's theme.
The score is lush
and soft
and warm
and deep
And the unknown is unholy
But clear blue.

In the movie of my mind
that drive is filled with the momentum of
everything coming next,
and the decision I made as a child
that I would not be a victim to myself
and the audience's knowledge
that if the hero wasn't going to make it,
they wouldn't still be watching.

The psych ward

is probably not
hidden behind a trick wall
just off the main lobby of the hospital
that they roll back like a stage set
after I admit my self,
this seventeen-year-old clutching a stuffed elephant
But that's what I remember.
And that's what my head felt like,
like someone was rolling back trick walls
off the main halls.
They let me hold my elephant
but everything else has to go.
I am given blue socks.
A hospital gown.
A plastic dog-tag for my wrist
in this place where every object has thought of
how you could use it to kill yourself
and has reshaped itself accordingly
and so you have zero chance of dying
Although a fair chance of not knowing who you are.

The psych ward

is sanitized
from more than germs
and mostly vacant,
either because they keep the rest of us
somewhere else, or 7 a.m.
on a cloudless July morning
is an unusual time to self—

. . . . *disintegrate?*
I try to hold aspects of my self
tied down to the main frame as I sit
on the examining table.
If I loosen my grip, one or two
could bob against the ceiling.
Not free, but just high enough
that I'll never reach it.
Nurses ask questions.
I am very scared that if a piece bumps them
they might catch it
and tell me I can't have it back.
I give them cliff-note answers.

Chromosomes unravel while they change
and at one point are not particularly anything.
—You're wearing scrubs. You understand chromosomes.

They ask if I tried to kill my self.
I tell them no.
They are confused.

The psych ward

is a picture of yourself
in the way they look at you.
They offer me a room and a bed
to wait while the ER psych comes
and decides what to do with me.
I am probably more afraid of them,
I am probably more of what they see
every day and certainly
not the worst of it

but they do look scared.
Their pupils widen to be big enough
to swallow mine. They give me a
feeling that they are seeing
something that they haven't before.
Please don't tell me what the others told me,
I pray. Please don't tell me
You're a good kid, you eat your
vegetables and know how to talk so
you will be alright.
Because I have been eating my vegetables
and talking my whole life but

I am not alright.
I am here.
I don't remember
if there was an IV or a pill. I remember
probably Mom's hand touching me,
and stirring inside the sock of my skin
in the after-sizzle of some tranquilizer

thicker than anything I've been given before.
It's time to go, my skin feels strange,
back through the trick wall and into the lobby,
where I focus very carefully
on remembering how to swallow
and not choking on the cup of water I'm handed.
I wave at a face I know.

The stranger smiles
Sadly.

Footnote

—destruct.
Not disintegrate.
Self-destruct
is the phrase.

But it wasn't like that.
There were no bombs or blood.

There was just space.
Widening.

Like the big bang from dreams of eons past
Is all true and inside of my atoms and cells

And my logic and longing,
And delicate particles of true me

Are beginning to pull from the bones
Of molecules

Like balloons snagged in a breeze.
Not out of spite,

Or hate,
But because their gravity

Is draining away elsewhere.

The ER psych

is very amused by me,
and I am very amused by him.
I think he likes that I don't curse him out
or fight him.
And I think he also is intrigued by the awkward angles
at which I poke out of the unchecked boxes
like I am some sort of mysterious creature
he has yet to encounter
in his long safari of insanity
and I am alright with that.
I have come here for rest
and some time before the drugs
come and place me somewhere else

there is so much rest in this man
sitting in a chair across from my bed
holding a clipboard he has already read
and doesn't look at as he tells me
that I am "amazing."
For the first time
in my weary little life
it's not patronizing to hear the doctor say that.
It's not to tie my uncut wrists
in the shiny nihilism of luck.

We talk for a long little time.
He's good for conversation
and one of my gifts is that after four days without sleep
I am still good for conversation, too.

"Do you have a therapist?" he asks.
I do not.
"You need one."
"Could you be my therapist?" I ask.
"You want me to be your therapist?"
"Well if that was an audition it was a pretty good one." In my memory my voice is a slurred and whimsical thing, I'm nearly a woman but for every night I don't sleep a few years get peeled off and I have been peeled back to just eight years old.
He doesn't answer right away,
and a few days later, another psychologist would tell us that
oh sorry, that one doesn't take private clients,
but in that moment, when I was this eight-year-old little girl in a hospital bed

he gives my mom a card
and a number
and a name

that I wish I remembered.

The Unicorn

"Well, we threw them a unicorn," says the head therapist
at the rehab program they've sent me to,
closing the door behind her as she
steps into the office
where I wait. Because I'm not like
the others.
I smile.
I smile, I behave, and also
I talk. The nurses smile so big
both times they take my blood pressure and weigh me
and the numbers aren't under or over. I wear clean,
brightly colored clothes—
I am clean. I am in color.

And that is very out of place.

Partial Hospitalization

In high school
they tell us that people don't kill themselves.
They die from mental illness.
Like mental illness is leukemia
or the flu.
It's nobody's fault, they say.
Nobody can control it,
and then they give us a short list
of things we can do to try anyway.

I had nightmares where it was like the flu.
It was airborne.
I watched it take people.
A virus with some vague
autonomy of its own
while apparently its victims didn't have any.
The episodes thickened and I was afraid
of the virus coming for me.

Your political correctness is an insult to me.

Pacing in Circles at 3 a.m.

What are you, You are your mind and your body But then why do both of those things seem to be working against you When you think about it In modern society "You" are what you can control You identify as what you can control There's this fault line There's this suture along your consciousness between what parts of your consciousness you can control and what parts of your consciousness you are just subjected to *Ugh* I keep using the word you when I actually mean I, I mean me, myself, my self my selves and I, It's annoying when people say you and us and they actually are just speaking for themselves (their self?) but to say *I am not totally in control* is so much more vulnerable than saying *You are not totally in control*—and look, imaginary friend or ex or celebrity or person I am jealous of that I have conjured to rant to—you are not in control either, but that's not the point, the point is that

When I talk with my hands

And look at the world with my eyes, and smile at you

From across the way

Those things all seem connected to
Who I actually am.

But then there is my heartbeat
Racing ahead without waiting for me to catch up.
At 3 a.m. there is the string of my thoughts
Unraveling into dark, threadbare fibers.
And while I would think

I am made of my thoughts,
My thoughts are much more like my heartbeat
Than they are like my hands
Inasmuch as I can control them.

I'm not sure if the difference
Is a boundary
Or a spectrum.

A Journal Entry

Whenever I have a thought that makes me uncomfortable or self-conscious I stab it with I HATE MY LIFE I HATE MY LIFE I HATE MY LIFE

but that's actually not true.
I don't hate my life.
I love my life.

I feel that I Suck
at this life that I so love.

Alright

I was holding on to *It's Going To Be Alright* like a toddler's blanket that was beginning to fray at the edges from so many washes and so much dragging it everywhere but denying all the holes and stains because I love it too too much to throw it away I've had it for my whole known consciousness and I just don't know what I would do if I got rid of it and so it's not in that bad condition, not really, it will still be another few months before the seams really come apart and hell, even years after they do I am that child who will still believe in it's going to be alright and take it with them wherever they go

When it is just rags.

No-Man's Land

The Problem

was that I was so much more suicidal
than I would admit to my self,
but I couldn't admit it,
I couldn't form it into words because I was also
nowhere near as suicidal as they all thought I was.

I am by principle terrible at secrets.
I know I have never kept anyone's secrets as well
as the ones I kept
from my self.

Suitcoat

My great aunt died in a car accident on the way
to my grandfather's funeral.

It was a sunny day. It had even been an alright one.
I was young. I did not understand death
because no one does,
but the ground was laid open to my father's father
with that green burial turf
like welcome mats
and we breathed easy in the ache
of heaven's paradox,
of the coming and going
that is home,
that is the way of us.
In big families, someone always has to be away.
Someone screamed horribly
a sound like her name
and that scream spread
the way we are taught kindness does in middle school.

But I don't remember feeling any of that.
What I remember feeling is

my Dad's suitcoat.
As he pressed me
into his chest, asking
If I was okay
A reverent black so it held
as much of the sun as a jacket
Could hold,

And the smell of cheap soap
from hotels
He had to travel far away to
for business trips,
Where I would miss Him whether I realized it or not
And where He would always miss me
And definitely realize it
And this scent—which He brought back home
in duffel bags and suitcases and would fill drawers with
For us to use, like some small apology
that He had to be away—
I realize now
I loved
And still do

Because it was the smell that He would always
Come home.
And that when He wasn't,
He thought of me.

Dialectics

the head therapist says,
is holding two opposing ideas in the same hand
at the same time.
You can be too warm
but want the comfort of a blanket,
in the midst of heartbreak
you can like the hurt,

"You can want to die
and also want to live," she says.

Bluebird // Peter Pan

They draw back a curtain like therapy
is a magic act
and reveal a wall of shelves
holding a whole library of fragile things.
Tourist keepsakes, ornaments,
antiques and figurines,
the random and curated curio shop
that is trauma and healing.
I notice

a small bluebird
guarding her egg in her nest
and I place her in my sandbox.

The others go back and forth between their sandboxes and
the shelves, editing and revising their stories with dozens
of symbols like they are foraging a language for the illiteracy
of pain while I

curl my knees
beneath me
and gaze at my mother bird.
And I think about playing Wendy
in eighth grade
and Thomas Bailey
and Peter Pan
the funeral home
and the cast list
and the part of the story when the high tide is gently swelling
beneath him
and he doesn't have a boat

and just as he begins to wonder
at the adventure of death—

this small mother bluebird
lends him her nest
and floats him
across the lagoon
and I think about Your face,
and the sharp fluorescent lights of the hospital
gleaming wetly in Your eyes
as You curl onto the hospital bed with me
and for the first time, let Yourself
cry, like how did we get here
like how did it get to this
but while Wendy and the lost boys and the pirates
are able to escape the lagoon
Peter can't

and You stay.

The Unicorn II

For years, it has seemed
that being the goody-two-shoes
of the depressed club means
that I am special, and alone.

It is nice to be special until it is not.
It is terrifying to be alone.

Have you noticed? How nothing
is really so terrible so long
as you're not alone?

Some nights when the sleeplessness
feels less like the lack of a thing and more like
a presence with teeth,
I go lie on the floor of my sister's bedroom
where just the idea of her
worn like a perfume on her carpet and walls
is enough to ward off the ghosts.

Most doctors don't know what to make of me,
and I don't know what to make of myself either.

I need help, but I don't belong.
That scares me.

All the same, I don't want to belong here.
No one does.

The clipboards at the hospital
are searching for malfunction
more than they are for pain.

To be told that you are special,
that there is a specialhood to be had.

That is when suicide starts to feel
something like natural selection,
which feels something like waiting
for the bear to decide
if I'm food or not
when I know my blood
smells the same as anyone's.

One of the counselors tells Cassandra
she needs to gather in with the group
for me to present my sandbox.
She is sitting slumped against the far wall,
looking as tired as a new mother,
more tired than death,
as tired as birth.
I tell her that she's fine where she is.
We meet eyes.

Dialectics II

On one hand:
"the bipolar" is not me.
It's just chemicals in my brain.

On the other hand,
Problem:
So is everything.

"I am not my mind"—a very useful mantra.

Except,
Um.

of course I am.

Fresh Air

In the Victorian era
fresh air was the cure-all
for everything.
Typhoid?
Breathe easy
and an extra dose of sun.
Tuberculosis?
Go sit in a cave
and the cool air
will rinse out your lungs.
Scarlet fever?
Take leave to the shore
and let the wind sweep
some spare color into your cheeks.

All those people died of course.

So am I naive to think
sitting here
with the existentialism scraping out
the insides of my head
leaving the bone raw and my nerves screaming bright static
against the backdrop drowning of people I don't know
and all their things that I don't care about
tripping my lungs like smoke—

that if I can just get out of this place
if I can just
breathe
the
dusk,
and sip at the sky,
I'll be alright?

The Victorians may have been wrong,
but I say they were onto something.
They were on the cusp of something great,
something *true*—
and then they all died.

Porch Light

Fate is all about angles.
At 4 a.m., when I am beginning to admit
that I have lost the night,
but still mourning it in the stifle of my sheets,
it is fixed at just such an angle
to pierce through my window's corner of evergreens
maybe a quarter mile away.
My bed is at just such an angle
to catch the glow on my pillow.
If my bed were anywhere else,
I would have never seen it.
In the daylight that house is nothing.
I couldn't even point it out to you.
At 4 a.m., I think about the people I've never met
and the hours they'll never know
I've spent
Gazing at the light they left on
To stay the night with me.

Antidepressant

I come home to my brain
to find I am locked out.
Daylight robbery.
Skeleton key.
Fists against the door,
shrill unarmed screams,
police are never near this part of town,
and if they were they wouldn't help me.
I'm thinking I could sit here
with my teenage fists and wait
for the fight to come to me.
But they also might starve to death
in spite,
and the doors would still be locked
from the inside.

Greek Gods

The thing about pills
is that some of the gods who give them to you
have no idea what it's like to be on them.
To fill your blood with demonic angels
and angelic demons,
sweeping out far corners of your consciousness—
the ones too tight for you to clean yourself—
sometimes pocketing the pieces
of you they find
for themselves:
Things you don't need,
Things you do.
Some Things you want
either way.

All of which
can sometimes make it hard to trust
the gods
who are of the Greek variety
Messy
warm and harsh and
passionate and pushy and
Removed,
just making mistakes like you and I,
just Human
except with Power
to boot.

Descartes

I just don't want to be a zombie,
I sob into the phone
on a crisp guest bed
in a very nice beach house
I wish sorely I could enjoy
Cling-wrapped in the sticky sheen
of some new, alien dosage,
Sucking on cellophane
and through the plastic I can see feelings
that I can't touch
This pill is a straitjacket
that doesn't keep me from writhing
I claw at the packaging to make air-holes—
The psych doesn't usually take calls on Sundays.

You are not going to be a zombie,
she promises.
We are going to find your Real Self.

My Real Self.

. . . What is that?

Who is she?

What is she like?

What of all This
Is she not?
Does she care
about me, and if so

Why has she left?

Where has she gone?

And is she coming back.

I can't answer any of those questions right now.

But I believe in my Real Self.
The way I believe in ghosts,
the way I believe in God.
There are many nights
it is easier to believe in the reality of a God
than a reality of myself.
But just the fact
That she can be referred to

seems to mean she must be real.
Even if I have no idea what she's like, I do know
that this here
is not real me,
And just that the disparity is felt
the deduction follows that somewhere

I must exist.

Cogito ergo sum.
I think, therefore I am.
Before it was a premise
I think it was a prayer.

II.

survival log

DAY 1
I Am an Opioid

Disclaimer:
I have never tried heroin.

But I remember that night,
Flitting around a dingy bar
packed past fire code
or comfort, and so thick with amps
I couldn't make out my own voice
Having just discovered the universe
and slipped it into my pocket
Feeling strong and ingenious
and unbreakable compared to the drink-stupored crowd
Sitting in the drench of amps
In a dingy bar
On a Wednesday night—
I didn't feel like I was actually in the room.
I was everywhere else.
I was outside my body
when I took an inventory of my nervous system
and thought,

This is chemical.

This isn't healthy.

Other people

Don't feel this way.

Physics

For every action
there is an equal and opposite
reaction.

The
pendulum
swings
toward
one
direction
and
it hovers there
for just a second,
gathering energy
before it
drops
toward
the
other

and
I
am
a
string

pulled
or
pulling.

DAY 2
Strayed

I didn't sleep at all last night.

I'm not terrified yet.
I'm spooked.
I'm off-trail, but it hasn't been long
and if executive functions
and the perceiving of time
and the volume of my thoughts in proportion
to my skull—
are trail mix and band-aids and water,
I have okay supplies.

But my head
is packed
past fire code or comfort
and I can't find
my own voice
in the drench of the amps, and as exhausted
as I am,
I'm still not sleeping

and that's when the trees all start to look alike.

Ode to Peanut Butter

In the daylight it would be a lustful
and gluttonous
and carnal thing to do, but at 3:46 a.m.
when I am physically a puddle of sleep drugs
and mentally a war zone of wants,
and think I may be getting maybe
almost somewhere a little bit closer
to unconsciousness
but the light across the street is flickering
and I just need a break from the sweat of my sheets

I take my stuffed elephant with me
as I hobble against the railing
to the kitchen
Don't turn on the light
and pat around the dark pantry shelves
until I find the jar
I get a spoon
and hope that no one is woken by the jangle of the drawer
and curl up on the couch
and lick it clean as long as I need to
until the fat works its way into my nerves
and I can go upstairs
and keep trying.

My Parents Are Not Home

My Father is far away.
They went on a trip.
They left just as all of this started.
They didn't know—I didn't know.
I want them to know
That I can do this.
That I can survive even
When They are away from me.

DAY 3
Wallow

There is a very fine line
Between admitting to the sad feelings
So that you don't blow up
And not wallowing in them
So that you don't fall apart.

Cold water

shocks out of the shower head and into my nerves
like jumper cables connecting to a dead engine.
At three days
I am not, strictly speaking, alive.
Most people don't think of sleep like oxygen or food.
Normal people think of sleep as something mystical and infinite.
But to bipolars it is something like fresh water.
It is finite. It is precious. It comes from the heavens.
It is sacred. It is baptism, and the pipes can run out of it.
I have not sipped *a dreg*
for three days

so I force myself to freeze under the faucet
for a solid minute,
because I'm going to school.
I'm in this mess because I got excited to present a project
and I need the insanity to mean something.
I am not asleep but I am not awake either.
The world is shimmering in a horrific way.
The ground of consciousness is shaking.
I slip into my seat.
I am about to start crying.
The teacher is looking at me.
Function is breaking down.
Three days' worth of pressure
is about to erupt right here in class.
This was wrong.
Swallow
Breathe
Zip the suit, I'm dying

I'm dying I'm dying I'm dying
I'm dying *Mr. Rosenthal, just so you know*
I don't feel good—

Mr. Rosenthal points to a poster.

"No excuses.

If you say you can't do it,
you can't.
But if you say you can
you can.
It's all about attitude.

It's all in your head, right?"

DAY 4
The Little Voice in My Head

The pill starts at the outskirts.
I feel a tad heavier
on the pillow.
It works its way in.
Closing my eyes feels easier,
the tense of my body loosens.
It gets into the thick of the fight.
My breaths are long
rolling hills, my nerves are
liquid, maybe I forget that I am
trying to sleep and am not

and then it arrives at the little voice in my head.
This minute militant murmur
that will not sink
into the black sand of sleep.
Bombshells backfire.
This little voice is running the show.

The psych-vetted, combat-ready, purple-hearted war general
is out of its depth.

She must be answered.
She must be wrestled.
She must be contended
by cognizance like herself,
She must be prayed for
and told she is loved.
She must decide that she is safe.

If you asked me when I was twelve, my true self
is all the things that succumb,
because sleep is what I want.

Lying here now, I think different.

The right pill

may control

what you honestly

Cannot.

But eventually

the battle arrives

upon what only you can

and don't know how to.

To Die, To Sleep

Madness sets in like dust.
Invisible debris that gathers
in cracks and corners of all the clocks.
I don't know what time it is.
I know that it is dark,
and my bed has become a place of pain,
and now I stagger through shadows
after vague motivations
Another pill
A drink of water, a drink of
Water and I will sleep, Another pill—
Did I already take another pill?
If I take two will I die?
If I don't take any I surely will
My limbs are drenched in drugs like clothes in water
How many pills have I taken now?
My neurons are fraying, fraying, fraying and
sprinting, sprinting, sprinting
Falling apart as they run
I pause against the doorframe of the bathroom.
Maybe I am about to die anyway.
My cheek presses against the wall
like Hamlet at the top of Act III.
"To die," he recites,
"To sleep." *Maybe sleep is here*
standing up against the wall.

Maybe sleep is here.

It is not there.

Maybe sleep is here.

It is not there.

Maybe sleep is here.

Tears.

". . . To be or not to be—
that is the question."

Dying sounds easier than this.

It is only a thought.
It creeps from beneath the edges of shadows.
The shadows vibrate.
The silence of the house resonates
With a dim heartbeat.
Sleep is not against the wall where Hamlet recites.
I follow a pulse across the hallway,
I find the edge of the banister, and my feet
Feel the shapes of stairsteps

To where deep in the heart of the night,
the blankets of my Parents' bed
Buoy
with soft, limber breaths.
My younger siblings are curled
in a cozy heap. I crawl
from the foot of the bed
and into their ridges.
The blankets are warm from them.
Like a suitcoat left in the sun.

For the first time in four very,
Very long days,
I let myself cry.
I realize
that I am not going to sleep tonight.
I try not to hyperventilate at the terror
of a fifth day.
I don't know that I have ever done a fifth day before.
I know the ins and outs of others,

but I don't know that I have ever been
to this particular circle of hell.

But tomorrow my Parents will be home.
Their bed smells like them.
I slip my hand into my sleeping sister's
and squeeze.
She does not squeeze back.
But she is holding me there.
All my kites have decayed
and the feeling of her skin is the only string
tying me to the earth.

No excuses.

If you say you can't,
you can't.

But if you say you can do it,
you can.

It's all about attitude.

It's all in your head,

Right?

DAY 5
Kitchen Light

You need four things to survive.

Air.
Water.
Food.
And Sleep.

I have not slept for five days.

My soul rolls
out of a stupored shell
that is too tired to move
but after hours
Hours
and hours and hours and hours and hours
And hours is not tired enough
to sleep.
Rolls off the couch in the dark
empty basement and army-crawls
across the floor
groping for where a door is
wondering if it is 6 p.m. or 2 a.m.
and my soul finds the railing of the stairs
and grips it
and drags empty limbs
up the staircase
where there is a slice of kitchen light

bleeding through the crack of the door
and the warm, faint shuffle
of Voices

that I know.

III.

waking up

Three things are true.

1. No one
   Can control all of themselves.

2. Everyone
   Can control some of themselves.

3. Whether you are a case study in the basement
   Of the psych ward
   Or a CEO at the front of the free world
   Because you are a Person
   Those first two things

   Never change.

Waking Up

I don't remember falling asleep.

I remember the rhythm of Dad's reading
like the litany of rain against a window
His voice
in the dewy lamplight of his bedroom

And then I turned gently
in the deep pillows of my Parents' bed.

Eyelids slowly blink apart
against pale, soft light
stretching through the window

And it is quiet.
The morning is deep,
and the house is a lush,
morning silence.

I am quiet.

My bones
Are quiet.

My neurons
Are still.

The whole world
Is quiet. And I realize

That I slept.

The tears are slow.
They are warm.
I realize
That I am here.
That I have come back
To my body.
Waking up
after five days without sleep
Is warm bread
after famine for a month and a half
Is cool water
after sweating your soul through your skin
for a day and a half
Is a breath
on the shore,
after choking on salt
for a minute

and a half.

But if you don't know what any of those are,
then Waking Up
is coming Home
after a very long trip
to find that
You still exist.

Insomnia is like throwing up

in that each time it happens,
it is so much worse
than my memory could capture
from the last time
I had to do this.

And also in that
I'm not sick because
I'm throwing up; I'm throwing up
because I'm sick.
This is not the disease.
This is what my imperfect being does
to purge it.

It's disgusting,
but afterward
I feel clean.

Awake // Survivor

I'm an ace student
and I just failed a math test
and in no close race
but with an extra hour of time after school and still
only chicken scratch
and finally a note in the corner, that
I'm sorry
I can't do this

—and I don't even care.

I don't care!
I cry twice a day because the aftershocks
of my decayed attention span are so sore
And it's beautiful,
and it's so humid my hair is sticking to my back
And it's beautiful
and my ride is late so I wait an hour with nothing to do
And it's beautiful to just be alive.
It's beautiful to just be feeling.
The sky is beautiful.
The clouds are beautiful.
The air is beautiful.
The way the cars drag on the air
as they rinse down the road and how the leaves
flicker against the shallow breeze is
all so beautiful, it's beautiful
to just be aware of it all.
It's beautiful to just be feeling.
It's beautiful to just be whole

even if in the most broken sense of whole
there is.

When you're deprived
of your Needs
for so long,
and then you're not,
you realize what you actually need
and what you don't
and that everything you don't can't hurt you
and that so little is important
and so much is beautiful.

My Inheritance

If you go down the road of my heritage
if you start at the edge of my driveway
and take a left at the first stop sign,
two rights and then another left,
you'll come to a yellow newspaper clipping
Bruised with that antique typeface
that had to be set into the press painfully
letter by letter,
bruises that read,
J. O. Jellison
was publicly declared insane
and sent to the institution.
Then if you come back up the way you came,
next to that first stop sign,
if you shake your fingers through the weeds at the base,
you'll find me sitting between an office's gray walls
at the age of eleven
or twelve
and will hear a stranger ask my mother if I have
any family history
of mental illness
and if you could time-travel as my genes have done
you would hear me hear her
recount
the darknesses my father's father
kept in his pockets,
a woman who fell through my cracks
and between children had a nervous breakdown
"—which she never quite recovered from."

The part of a daughter's inheritance that you give her as a child
is the belief that everyone deserves to be known,
the way her grandfather was known
to make friends with everyone.
You teach her to sing loud in church
and play on the piano
that four generations ago a mother commissioned
sometime before or after the asylum.
You don't tell her the records of hospitals
turned to folklore,
the screams passed down in whispers,
the things a nurse curled through her typewriter.
You can't.

But I, the young heiress,
came upon that safe
with all its codes curled in my fingerprints.
And that gray office is not the most this has ever hurt
but that may have been the moment that it all scared me
the most,
to look upon this inheritance
and wonder
what terrors
had been laid aside
ahead.

My grandfather didn't know that I was bipolar before he died,
no one did,
but I think now he does.
I think he may have gotten word
before I did.

Time-traveling the way that genes do,
writing things that we can't know
the meanings of when they are written
in long thin painful strings
of letter by letter,
and then tucking those futures
somewhere along the brown backroads
of the past—

he penned me a note
that he must have forgotten to send
but that arrived from my grandmother
long after he was buried.
Not in typeface, but handwritten
in the shapes of his voice
saying,
little girl,
this is a scary time to be alive
but you're gonna make it.

And that was my inheritance too.

IV.

heritage

Genocide

For centuries, my people were locked away
into brick jails of mixed intentions
where they were deprived and depraved
And dead
because they were different.

That was our genocide.

And now we DIY insanity for Halloween
Wear an ax on a headband like some cuckoo had a bad day
Tragedies marketed with the likes of Frankenstein's
and Dracula's and Mr. Hyde's
More monsters to be fascinated by
More horror stories
Teenagers break into their mass graves,
the asylums that offered no asylum
From demons
That they will try to prank
Disturb the vegetables
Maybe they'll get lucky
Maybe they'll catch a ghost
Or if nothing else a thrill
Isn't it exciting how much suffering and death happened here,
Isn't it neat that it's so strong that centuries later
you can still feel it in your skin
just standing there?

That was my genocide.
People make a commodity out of it.

We imagine

that those people
who talked to walls for hours
and chased delusions in the dark
and were strapped to beds
and hosed down
and straitjacketed
and had their brains nibbled by doctors' dirty fingers

Were some sort of Mythical
Monstrous
Incurable insanity

But they weren't.
A lot of them were bipolars.

They were human beings just like me.
If I had lived then, I may have been just like them.

This Still Bugs Me

One time in an English class
the discussion had somehow strayed to depression
and a classmate who probably genuinely did
think he knew what he was talking about
remarked how terrible it was to think
that the whole time Robin Williams was laughing
and singing and performing for us, the whole entire time
he was actually dying on the inside

And I don't know Robin Williams,
so I can't speak for the guy

But that's not how bipolar works.
All the laughs Robin gave us were totally real
or we wouldn't have felt them.
When Marilyn charmed the silver screens,
she found joy there.
Even if he was a lion at rehearsals,
Beethoven must have reveled in holding a concert in his hands
or he could not have pushed through deafness to feel it.

And when I call your name
and skip down the sidewalk to catch up with you
and demand the details of your day,
I am not hiding that I was in a funk last week.
I am just genuinely overwhelmed to see your face.

We are not horror stories.
I may have had more sadness in my life than some,
but it doesn't mean that I've had any less joy.

Dialectics III

Does bipolar disorder pose a challenge for artists
or fuel their creativity?
an old newspaper article asks.
(Paraphrase question—
Everyone keeps asking.)

Yes.

Starry Night

to me was always about
how warm and safe the little town looks below,
how warm and safe
their little worries and dreamfuels are,
in their pretty shapes that hold themselves.
Compared to the vast
and frigid manic sky,
bright to see but cold to touch.
Some people say
Van Gogh's sky is literally manic.
Literally what he saw
in his psychotic throes.
I think it is more what I feel
from the inside of the undertows
of dark and light. I've never seen
the graveyard cypress in the foreground
as much as the steeple
tiny and cold and trying to touch
Divinity.

A Friend

It's odd
to read a canned textbook definition of what bipolar is
beneath a photo of Virginia Woolf
written by someone who clearly
knew nothing about what bipolar is
or what I have been through
But to look at her,
and to think,

She Did.

Humans

We press shells
to our ears
and hear the long shadow of our blood's
tiny flutter
threading life through our lacework
and think—
It is the ocean.
Calling us.

Churchill Called It His Little Black Dog

I wonder if he took it on walks.

I wonder if it followed him to work
or if he left it at home and locked the doors.

I wonder if it ever ran away
and how often and how long
could be expected before it came back. Surely it had a bite—

I wonder if it bit because it was mean
or just because it was afraid,
and I wonder if it was really that little
or if it was just that the person who had enough steam for Hitler
could fit a timber wolf
in a purse. If it was just
that the person who was haunted by a timber wolf
could certainly fight a Hitler.

A dog is an apt expression
for a.k.a. "manic depression"
because it's when dogs get excited
that the leash snaps back.
It's when they get depressed that they
bite harder.

Heritage

Being sick is not a superpower.
Dying on the inside is not some noble battle that must be fought
for the greater good of the art.
Hollywood makes insanity look noble the way
Victorian ads sold war as adventure.
It's not.
It's not an escapade or exploit.
It's ugly,
and even if the halls of her mind that made madness
were connected to the halls that made beauty
if Virginia Woolf had not put rocks in her pockets
and stepped into a river
she would have lived
to make much much more,
and the genetic deck is not rigged so perfectly
that in order to get all the aces
you must also get the duds.
Pain is not prestigious
Madness is not a contingency of greatness
Insanity is not a prerequisite for genius

—But I do hope to be among the geniuses
since I have had to be among the insane.

And I feel pride in my heritage.

I feel like they are watching.

I feel connected to them.

I am grateful for their noise.

I feel a horizon of expectation.

Not of greatness,
Or legacy or fame,

But of creation.

To rise
And create
In Spite Of It All.

V.

autonomy

Texts

i went on a walk and i'm a little bit
lost in the woods

i'm trying to follow maps

i can see where i am headed
in relation to where i entered the woods
but if i go off the path and beeline
i will probably just get lost?

Past Midnight on My Cousin's Bedspread Rambling About the Nature of Autonomy and All the Things I'm Gonna Do About It

"Can you tell how manic I am right now?"

"Not really. You just seem like you."

I prop up on an elbow to look at her. "But right?
But exactly.
It's just me.
Whenever I come out to someone about being bipolar
they're like, I never would've guessed that,
you don't seem like that,
and it's because they don't actually know
what bipolar disorder is
and they've never known a bipolar person before
but it's also because they imagine
that there's like this little monster
I'm hiding in the closet.
But there's no monster.

It's just me."

WARNING LABEL
(Please read.)

Do not be a human or take one in unless you are prepared
to meet said human's excessive needs. Urgent needs may include
(but are not limited to):

Oxygen
Water
Shelter
Rest
Means of warmth
Calories
Carbs
Fats
Proteins
Vitamins
Salt
Regularly seeing the sun
Defense mechanisms
Some means of communication
A few people whom the human loves
and who in best cases
(most cases)
Love the human too.

Each human also comes with another class of needs,
some of which are not urgent, but *VERY important.*
Examples include
(but are not limited to):

Seeing the ocean regularly

A wheelchair
Extra space
Time to oneself
Pictures of the sky
An interpreter
A walking cane
Prayer
Other people's prayers
Long hugs
Favorite books
A certain voice
Sunrises before work
Running shoes
Hot showers
Physical therapy
Behavioral therapy
Good movies
A prosthetic
Scriptures
Laughter
A musical instrument

Lithium.
Lamotrigine.
Seroquel.
Vraylar.
Hydroxyzine.
Abilify.

And Klonopin
(For sleep.)

Each human is Designer-made (by Hand).
Handle with care at all times.

Product is more fragile than may appear.

Diagnosis

Once upon a time
an author was accused
of his books not fitting
a genre.
He replied that genres are for bookstores.
When enough books have enough similarities
a genre is born
and naming genres helps us find
the things we are looking for.
But the Author
did not write his books
according to the dimensions
of a genre.

Genres are real.
But you are not a genre.
You are a book.

Holy Things

Emotions are never wrong.

Observations can be wrong.
Expressions can be wrong.
Obsessions can be wrong.
Fixations can be wrong.
Actions can be wrong.
Reactions are often immoral
Opinions can be flat-out incorrect
And most words are generally untrue,
in some way or other,

But emotions are holy things.

Bipolar Disorder

Is brain cells swallowing more sodium than they know
what to do with

But it's also a feeling,
like the whole world is your problem to solve
and you can't sleep until you do.
Bipolar disorder

Is epileptic seizures manifested as oil paintings
and bad decisions

But it's also the porch light across the street
being the only one who understands you.
Bipolar disorder

Is a tug of war between brain receptors

But it's also falling in love
being your default. Kinetic energy
where others have a resting position.
Bipolar disorder

Is serotonin playing chutes and ladders

But it's also crying on the steps
after everyone else has left.
Bipolar disorder

Is flutters of microglia

and an immune system that is bad at homeostasis
and neuropsychiatric pathogenesis and other things
I can't pronounce, in fancy research papers
that I will never understand.

But it's also a supernatural stretch of space
between the parts of me I can control
and the parts of me I can't
but which are also
Who I am.
It is also the colors in shadows
and all of the things I am afraid of.

Dawn and Dusk

What we call sky
is actually just space.

And inside of you, there is lots of it.

It is filled with heat. It is filled with the trade winds
between your spirit and your blood.
In the contours of the pills, try to measure
the distance between you
and the ends of your nerves.
Between the skate of your neurons
and the voice in your head.
It is not unlike the space
between the pull of the moon
and the gravity of the sun.
A romance. An exchange of power.
A sort of dusk. A sort of dawn.

Everyone experiences this space that exists.
Everyone feels the shrug of the light on their skin.

But when you're peers with the stars
and your soul
is a sleepless creature
now sitting
on the back porch alone
the only one Awake
at the crack of morn—

the space feels wider.

The sunrise feels longer.
The tension of the Lights'
love affair
Feels deeper,
as they fight for autocracy of the sky.

Amid my high-noon fever dreams
    effervescing like sunsick phosphenes
and the moonless sobs of my psyche's psych ward
    creaking my chest like midnight floorboards

there is also this bleed.
Inside the tugs of night and day.
When the firmament that is my consciousness
is flooded by the light
that is my actual self.
Just raw color.
Roaring across the sky,
but also perfectly quiet.
Filled with a momentum
That is perfectly still.

And that space is sacred
To me.

In Case Nobody Told You

Not a single atom of your body
is touching.
You are held together
by just polarities
just rows and rows
of tiny controversies
forming seams—
We are not solid,
just resisting.

Dialectics IV

I have never regretted that I am this way.
I have never wished that I had been made differently.
I take my pills
and I hold them to my heart,
their canisters are like treasure chests
and I collect them like medals
and they are dayblood to me,
But there is also something hallowed
about the swing of the pendulum
about the weight of the drop
and the heat
and my bipolarness is not
Some segregated psych ward of my mind
behind a trick wall,
It is *part* of me.
It touches all of me.
The whole world is my psych ward.
My bipolarness is not some barbwired ghetto of my city
It is the graffiti
that grows like ivy down the blocks
It is the poetry
spray-painted in alleyways
It is the ultimatums of the marginalized
broadcast
on the brick
of the capitol building.
It is a sense.
It is a way I touch
and feel
and see,

Sometimes I think it is the part of me
that has made me
Me
the most.

I know myself inside and out
the way a detective knows the accused
From years of tracking them down.

Breathe in.

And when you do,
breathe in the stars.
Breathe in the amber exhales
of other worlds
that have wrinkled eons
to touch you. Breathe in
the embers
of another Time
blushing against yours
the light
that is shards of moments
glancing across the ether
like skipping stones
rippling our corner of the dark. Breathe in
the soft din
of novas crashing
millennia away
crumpling like dry leaves. Breathe in
the faint glow of distant gravities
and the tides of other galaxies
and the tides of your own
and the things that get lost in the surf.
Breathe in the frayed edge of the dusk
and the pull of the sun.
Breathe in everything
that you have ever loved.
Breathe in chocolate pudding
on Tuesdays in kindergarten
and paper dolls you made

with your sister
and the dress you wanted to wear every day
and the first chord
of your favorite song
and the dog-eared page of your favorite book
that was a feeling you had never
felt before. Breathe in
the fireflies you never caught
and the specific feel of your mother's shape
the first time the world
was unfair. Breathe in
the shatter of raindrops
against your cheeks
and the warm white noise
of your favorite street. Breathe in
your grandfather.
Breathe in his smile
and the worn edges of his laugh. Breathe in
the last words he said to you
the texture of the last syllables
he pressed into your palm.
Breathe in the worst day of your life
and the others that broke
like sunrises
against the sky of your nerves
Everything you've ever felt
and did or didn't deserve
shades of gray
between the black-and-whites
loves and fears
and wrongs and rights

that elsewhere
are a gasp.
A passing breath of light.

And then breathe out.
And give it all back.

Mania II

When I sojourn from my skin
to dance among the heavens
I believe there are angels
who as I float away
knot a string
around my ethereal ankle
and tie the other end
to my body
and even as I float, I stay anchored to myself
if by only a thread
and when it is time
for me to come home
they reel me in like a kite
and while I am out reaching for the moon
the angels watch over my precious
fragile shell,
and guard it from the ghosts.

Depression II

My wish for you
is that when it's all said and done
you have some corner of yourself
to come home to.
That is yours.
That the demons don't reach.
That is clean on messy days
and familiar in strange times
and that you can hang with photographs
of the moments and places
and voices and faces
that have collaged who you are.
That is kept warm with your past selves
like a hearth of hot coals
maybe not ablaze
but still burning
still glowing
casting shadows across the wall.

You can be living on Millionaires' Row
but we're all homeless
if we don't have that much.

To My Fellow Manic-Depressives

After Rudyard Kipling

If you can make hell breathable

If you can find a way from the inside
to poke air holes in the box
and in that tight little space can marshal
the traffic of your thoughts

If you can stay calm

If you can reach into your recesses of self
and find a scrap of truth
and from the shrapnel of past lives
build yourself anew

If you can do pain

If you can notice the beauty of the sun
even when your blood is a scream
and rise above the begs of your blood
to find what your blood means

And if you can make it all a song

Then there is nothing available to anyone else
Who has ever lived
That is not available to you
too.

You are not cursed.
Just because you're broken
Doesn't mean you're the victim,
and the Universe
Is your birthright to claim.

The Weeds // Graduation

I spend my first period
not in my first period
but in the woods
behind the school
tread my clean school shoes
on the dirt path damp with rain
carved through the trees,
manmade like all paths are
but overrun with wild things
overgrown with destinies
crowding the map like weeds

a trail I just recently realized existed
but in another life
I would have run these trails every beautiful day like this one
because I would have realized I love to run
a hot second earlier than I did
walking this one
and I would have joined cross country sophomore year
and been swallowed into Mia's other circle
and in another life
Thomas Bailey didn't kill himself
in eighth grade
and I was his first kiss
and he wasn't quite in Mia's circle
but they liked him.
Everyone did.
As in this life

I pluck a stray destiny from the side of the path
and breathe a wish,
and the petals that don't lift away,
I tease off myself.

Treading Water

Mental illness is like anything.

It takes practice.
There are the Dabblers—
who poke the water with their toes,
occasionally take a dip,
always shocked by how cold it is—
Then the Hobbyists—
who now and again swim laps,
know the form of each stroke
know how cold water feels—

and then there are the Professionals.

I have been swimming my whole life.
From the time I was five,
learned to tread water;
ragged kicks that wore through
my legs,
naive for the deep end
but Dad was always
just behind,
there was no chance of drowning
with Him there, His Fingertips
the smallest reach
from mine,
Even Stronger
in the water, where gravity
was so thin
and I weighed so little.

I quickly made the team
that shifted over the years,
and then sometime in my teens,
I began winning
Races—
that were against the statistics,
against Time,
but that only really mattered
and I only even tried in
because they were really just races
against myself.
The races got hard.
So did I. I didn't mind
my burning lungs
because if I could
just
kick
hard enough
I knew I could beat myself.

And these days
I am pretty much always at the pool.
(In some form or another.)
And as Professionals go,
I'm very good at what I do.
I take my pills.
I get my exercise.
I fight the mirror,
and eat.
I fight my gag reflex,
and eat.
I stay social.

I ask for help even
when the ghouls have crawled
through my ears with their lies.
I am charitable to the winter
when it has overstayed its welcome.
I take my deep breaths.
I notice the sky.
When purpose is in famine,
I pick the meat off the bones.
I bookkeep my seasons,
I harvest the good things,
I write my hard feelings
and my soft gratitudes.
I make space for the darkness
and I don't let it cheapskate the light.
Mental illness becomes a skill.
It just takes practice.
And practice doesn't make perfect,
but it makes us,
and there is a truth that is written
into muscle.
The secret belongs to no one.
Breath belongs to everyone,
and is yours to burgeon in your blood
to that place where gravity is thin
and breath is illicit.
I don't mind the cold water.
I warm up quickly.

. . . But you know something?
Even as a Professional
my lungs still burn
when I crawl the wall to the bottom of the pool
and they always will. Much less
if I train
but still.
Holding my breath will never feel comfortable,
no matter how many times I do it
and Even as a Professional

I still reach
for my Dad.
His Fingertips
the smallest reach
from mine
and in places too deep to touch,
He holds me.

Further Resources

Bipolar Disorder Hotline
https://mentalhealthhotline.org/bipolar-hotline

Depression and Bipolar Support Alliance
https://www.dbsalliance.org/support/for-friends-family/for-teens

National Institute of Mental Health: Bipolar Disorder in Children and Teens
https://www.nimh.nih.gov/health/topics/bipolar-disorder

National Suicide and Crisis Lifeline
https://988lifeline.org

Or call 988 for 24/7 confidential support

About the Author

Ella Grace Foutz grew up in Ohio as the middle child of a large family. Having struggled since the age of nine and after seeing clinicians for years, Ella was finally diagnosed with bipolar at the age of eighteen. It is her dream that this book will help make it easier for bipolar people to be diagnosed effectively, and more than that, teach those struggling that they are not alone. Ella has spent a great deal of her sleepless nights writing in her journals, and some of these poems come to you live from her experiences. When light is exhausting but her mind is still racing, she writes by hand in total darkness. She cannot always read it the next day. Beyond writing, Ella is also a passionate musician, distance runner, and believer in Christ. She is a graduate of Southern Virginia University with her bachelor's degree in liberal arts. Visit her on her Instagram @e.g.poetry. This is her debut book.